MW00472222

How to Break Curses

THE SIMPLE SECRET
HOW TO
UNLOCK GOD'S BLESSINGS

And Live A
CURSE FREE
BLESSED LIFE

Jim Kibler

ACKNOWLEDGEMENTS

Mary Kibler, my wife and ministry partner, for her suggestions, editing and support.

Jean Johnson, for her suggestions, editing and prayers.

Our Wonderful Church Family, for their support and encouragement.

My Prayer Partners, whom I pray with every day.

HOW TO BREAK CURSES

INTRODUCTION

I do not like this book. I don't even like talking about the subject of CURSES. Unfortunately, this book is very necessary. So many people, including most Christians, are living with CURSES that keep them sick and broke and create major problems in their lives.

You do not have to live with CURSES. You can live a BLESSED LIFE, completely unhindered by CURSES that block THE BLESSINGS of God. Let's start living a CURSE FREE LIFE BLESSED LIFE today.

RECOGNIZING CURSES

Do you feel like something is hindering your success, or keeping you sick? Have you been waiting for a long time for God's BLESSINGS to begin working in your life? Does it seem like there are obstacles in your path at every turn? Are your finances stymied and you never seem to be able to save any money?

Do you have enough to pay all of your bills? Is your life full of stress and you go from one crisis to another? Are you accident prone? Do you have relationship difficulties? Do you make bad decisions and have a hard time dealing with life in general?

If this is the case, I can guarantee that CURSES are operating in your life. The problem is in the spiritual realm and so is the answer.

INVISIBLE OBSTACLES

CURSES cannot be seen and that is why most people, including many Christians, do not even know that CURSES exist, let alone the fact that they are a very real dominating force in the lives of people. These same people wait years for God to BLESS them, or heal them, not knowing that INVISIBLE CURSES are blocking their healing. CURSES are also blocking THE BLESSINGS OF GOD from coming upon them. That used to be me. Not anymore.

The word CURSE, in all of its different forms, is found over 230 times in the Bible, yet is totally ignored by most churches and Ministers. Every Minister should be concerned with the affects that CURSES have on people.

CURSES control people, their lives, and their families.

Everyone is either BLESSED, or CURSED in every area of their life and also in their body. There is no in between.

The word BLESSED means to be spiritually programmed for a good, healthy, abundant and successful life. The word CURSED means to be spiritually programmed for a hard life, including chronic sickness, failure, poverty and destruction.

2

FOUR MAIN CATEGORIES OF CURSES

CURSES OF SIN, which started in the Garden of Eden when Adam and Eve ate the forbidden fruit.

CURSES OF THE LAW, which resulted from disobedience to the Law that God gave to Moses.

CURSES OF DISOBEDIENCE, which are a result of failure to obey God's Word.

SPOKEN CURSES, which are pronounced upon a person by themselves, or by someone who has spiritual authority over them.

Until Adam and his wife sinned in the garden, there was no such thing as a CURSE on the earth. The earth was a **CURSE FREE ZONE.**

There is no such thing as luck. You are either BLESSED, or you are CURSED.

THE BLESSING is something that comes upon you, pursues you and overtakes you. It causes you to live a wonderful, happy, stress-free life with good health, abundance and accomplishment. **A BLESSED LIFE.**

THE CURSE is something that comes upon you, pursues you, overtakes you and causes you to live a life of adversity, unhappiness, frustration, difficulty, hardship, stress, anxiety, fear, drama, no peace, no rest, suffering, sickness, and financial problems. **A CURSED LIFE.**

Unfortunately, there are a lot more people living THE CURSED LIFE, than living THE BLESSED LIFE, including many Christians.

DEFINITION OF A CURSE

A CURSE is permission for an evil spirit, or spirits, to legally enter into and operate indefinitely in the life of a person, or in a specific area of a person's life.

CURSES give unclean spirits, a legal right to steal, kill, destroy and bring torment into the lives of people, including Christians.

CURSES give continual permission for unclean spirits to hinder the health and life of a person, including finances.

CURSES can be acquired in a vast number of ways, many of which are outlined in this book.

God does not CURSE anyone, but there are times when He will refuse to BLESS someone, or will withdraw an existing BLESSING. When a BLESSSING is removed, a CURSE immediately comes in and occupies the space, either in the body of a person, or in their life.

I have heard people say that Christians cannot have CURSES. Not true.

When people become born again, the only CURSE that is removed is the CURSE OF SIN. Other CURSES will stay in the life of these good people and continue to operate.

If you have been struggling in any area of your life over a long period of time, be it your health or your finances, you can be 99.99% sure that CURSES of some kind are involved.

Look around in your own church, your neighborhood and place of business. If you see sickness, lack, poverty and strife you know that CURSES are involved. There may be some involved in your own life.

Everyone, in every area of their lives, is either BLESSED, or CURSED. A person's entire life can be BLESSED, or CURSED, or they can be BLESSED in some areas of their life and CURSED in other areas.

Many people wait years for God to BLESS them without ever realizing that CURSES are blocking THE BLESSING OF GOD from manifesting in their lives.

BLESSINGS and CURSES cannot occupy the same area of any person's life at the same time.

There is no natural remedy for CURSES. Since CURSES are supernatural, the remedy must also be supernatural.

An unhindered, CURSE free life will result in good health and wealth. Actually, the fewer CURSES that are operating in your life the better your health will be and the more you will live in abundance.

What I want to get across in this book is how easy it is to live A BLESSED, HEALTHY, and ABUNDANT LIFE. Actually, I intend for everyone who reads this book to begin living a productive, satisfying, stress free, abundant, healthy, BLESSED LIFE starting right now.

WARNING

Please be advised that it can be **very dangerous** to be casting CURSES and unclean spirits out of people before they know how to keep them out.

First of all, before any attempt at BREAKING CURSES, which also involves the removing of unclean spirits that are operating under the authority of a CURSE, a program of getting words under control **must be** undertaken.

Matthew 12:43 Jesus said, "When the unclean spirit is gone out of a person, he walks through dry places, seeking rest, and finds none. [44] Then he says, "I will return into my house from where I came out." When he is come, he finds it empty, swept, and garnished. [45] Then he takes with himself seven other spirits more wicked than himself, and they enter in and dwell there: and the last state of that person is worse than the first. Even so shall it be also unto this wicked generation."

According to Jesus, in this passage, when CURSES and evil spirits are cast out, they will try to get back in and if allowed to come back, will bring seven friends, (Other unclean spirits) who are even more evil that they are.

WARNING

A man, dying of cancer, sought me out. He said, "I am going to find Pastor Jim." He called someone who knew me and got my address. On a Wednesday evening, during our mid-week fellowship, he came in his pajamas and had members of his family carry him into the house, as he was too weak to walk. The CURSE was broken, the unclean spirits removed and he was completely healed.

His doctors and family then convinced him to enter treatment, "Just to make sure the cancer was gone." The cancer soon came back in a different area.

Six months later, he was again dying of this horrible disease. Hospice had even taken him off food and water to hasten his death. He had his daughter call me to come see him. Again, he was completely healed.

A year later, the cancer came back in yet another area. I went to see him without being called. I walked into his house and asked him what was going on. He said that he was full of cancer and the doctors said he only had two weeks or so to live. He said he was OK with that so I said goodbye and left without ministering to him at all.

I saw him six months later and he was fine. I asked him what happened and he said that after I left that day, he started feeling better and two weeks later, tests showed that his returning cancer was gone. Those evil spirits of cancer had left him when I walked through the door of his house. I believe it was the **same spirits of infirmity** that I had cast out of him twice earlier. They recognized me and fled. Several times in the gospels, the unclean spirits recognized Jesus and were afraid of Him.

HOW PEOPLE RECURSE THEMSELVES

I believe Jesus, when He said that after evil spirits are commanded to leave a person, they hover close by, waiting for an invitation to come back in. According to Jesus, they consider the body and the life of the person they were just cast out of to be their home.

The number one way that people allow CURSES back in is by RECURSING themselves with negative words.

The minute a person who has been delivered from a CURSE, RECURSES THEMSELVES with their words, the CURSE comes back and the returning unclean spirits will each bring 7 of their friends who are more wicked than they are. That person then be much worse off that they were before the original CURSE was removed. This is what we need to be very careful of.

I highly recommend, that before any deliverance of CURSES and accompanying unclean spirits is attempted, a program of watching your words is started. This is the most important thing you can do.

I am getting to the point where I want people to practice watching their words for 90 days before we start to break any CURSES that might be operating in their bodies, or their lives.

BE VERY CAREFUL

Ministers, be very careful when dealing with people who have CURSES operating in their lives. There is no room for error. If you make a mistake, the person will be much worse off than they were when you started.

Secondly, make sure people fill their spirit with God's Word at least some every day. That is why I absolutely insist that all of my prayer partners watch my 15-minute videos every day if they want me to pray with them on a regular basis. These short videos will increase their faith and strengthen their spirits.

Several years ago, we had a very nice lady come to our church. She had left a church, which was teaching what we call a false religion. She was sick, broke and alone. Within a year, she was healed, got a great job, met and married a wonderful man and was living a happy life of abundance.

After a year or so, she started coming to church only once in a while. Then she went back to her former church and within a few years, she was living in fear and was sick again. She lost her good job; her husband divorced her and finally she died a horrible death from cancer. The CURSES and unclean spirits had returned, only this time she was much worse off than she was the first time. None of her family, or friends have any understanding of what happened to her.

I do not fight against CURSES and unclean spirits. I break CURSES in THE NAME OF JESUS and I tell unclean spirits to shut up and come out. Before I do this for anyone, I want to make very sure they will not let them back in. Please go slow and be very careful.

HOW CURSES OPERATE

A CURSE is defined as an utterance intended to invoke harm, damage, or punishment on a person, or something. Being spiritually empowered to fail in the entire life of a person, or designated areas.

CURSES GIVE unclean spirits legal entry and continual permission to stay in a specified area of a person's life. That permission must be given by that person, a person who has spiritual authority, or by God.

When a person is under a CURSE, unclean spirits have a legal right to oppress them in designated areas of their life.

CURSES are like a wet blanket that constantly covers a person, or a dark shadow that hovers over them.

CURSES are BLESSING BLOCKERS. Derek Prince called them invisible barriers. He is right. I call them invisible obstacles.

CURSES are an invisible, supernatural force with the purpose of blocking God's BLESSINGS. The unclean spirits that accompany them, steal, kill and destroy in the lives of God's most treasured creation, His people.

All CURSES began when Adam and his wife sinned in the Garden.

No CURSE can ever enter any person's life without permission. Usually this permission is from a person, but there are some forms of behavior that cause CURSES to receive permission from God to come in and operate.

The force behind all CURSES is always unclean spirits. Jesus sometimes called them devils.

CURSES cannot be overcome, but they can easily be broken.

LEGAL RIGHTS

Revelation 3:20 Jesus said, I stand at the door and knock: if anyone hears my voice and opens the door, I will come in to them.

Jesus knocks on the door, ready to come in with with eternal salvation and the abundant life. The door must be opened and He must be invited to come in.

The devil also knocks on the door, with his CURSES and unclean spirits, ready to come in to steal, kill and destroy. The door must be opened and he must be invited to come in, or he must stay out.

CURSES open the door and give unclean spirits a legal right to come in. They will then stay in a person's life and cause destruction as long as THE CURSE remains in place.

All CURSES, no matter how they get into the life of any person, are accompanied by unclean spirits, whose only assignment is to steal, kill and destroy. John 10:10

Before any unclean spirits are cast out, CURSES which have given them the legal right to be there, must be broken, or they will not stay out.

As long as CURSES remain unbroken in the life of a person, unclean spirits have a legal right to come back, even if they have been cast out. Once the CURSE has been broken, the unclean spirits lose all of their legal rights to stay and oppress a person. They will leave and not come back. That is unless they are invited to come back in by the person's negative words.

Faith will temporarily override a CURSE, but to get substantial and lasting relief, THE CURSE and accompanying unclean spirits must be removed by someone with GREAT FAITH in the NAME OF JESUS.

CURSES can affect the inside, or outside of a person's body, or things concerning their life, especially their family and finances.

EVIDENCE OF A CURSE

- Chronic sickness and disease.

- Chronic financial problems.

- Chronic failure.

- Chronic fear, anxiety, depression and stress.

- Chronic relationship difficulties.

- Accident prone.

- Thoughts of suicide.

- Obesity.

- Repeated failure.

- Bad habits, including Gambling.

- Mental illness, including Alzheimer's and Dementia.

- Substance abuse, including alcohol, drugs and nicotine.

- Bad temper, mood swings and violence.

- Physical and mental abuse.

- Controlling behavior.

If any of these are also present in parents or siblings, they are GENERATIONAL CURSES.

CURSES can cause spiritual death, physical death, sickness, poverty, the hard life, fear, failure, loss, difficulties, and obstacles in the lives of people. Actually, everything bad that happens is from the devil and can usually be traced back to a CURSE of some kind.

UNNECESSARY SUFFERING

All CURSES cause suffering of some kind, but because Jesus redeemed us from THE CURSE OF THE LAW, all suffering caused by CURSES is totally unnecessary.

There are four forms of punishment for sin:

- Spiritual death. Paid for by the Blood of Jesus.
  Ephesians 1:7

13

- Sickness. Paid for by the stripes of Jesus. 1 Peter 2:24

- Poverty. Paid for by the poverty of Jesus. 2 Corinthians 8:9

- Hard life. Paid for by the crown of thorns. Matthew 27:29

DOUBLE JEOPARDY

CURSES give the devil a legal right to apply the same punishment for sin to people that was applied to Jesus when He paid the price and took the punishment for our sin. I call that double jeopardy.

The devil's objective is to make you suffer the same punishment for sin that Jesus suffered when He went to the cross. When Jesus said "It is finished" He meant total redemption. He does not need us to help Him by suffering the same punishments that He did. That would be double jeopardy.

DEMONS

Jesus called them devils and unclean spirits. Many people refer to them as demons, although that term is not used in the Bible. The Bible is not clear as to where they came from, so we do not know for sure. We do know that they oppress and sometimes even possess people.

All CURSES are accompanied by unclean spirits.

These unclean spirits cause sickness, disease and poverty. Their assignment is always the same, as the thief Jesus described in John 10:10 when He said, "The thief, (Any unclean spirit), comes to steal, kill and destroy."

Christians can be oppressed by unclean spirits but cannot be possessed because they have Jesus, in the form of the Holy Ghost, living within their spirits. People who are not born-again Christians can actually be possessed by these horrible things.

Unclean spirits cannot break into a person's life unless a CURSE, which gives them the legal right to be there, is present. The devil cannot just pick out people and send unclean spirits to attack them.

The assignment of every CURSE and all accompanying unclean spirits, is to steal, kill and destroy. When they get into a person's life through a CURSE, they will do just that.

There are spiritual laws governing CURSES and one of them is the fact that CURSES can only operate in a person's life if they have a legal right to be there.

The devil cannot inflict CURSES on anyone without permission.

CURSES cannot just come upon you for no reason and the devil cannot just use unclean spirits to attack any person that he wants to. People call me and say, "Pastor Jim, please help me, I am under attack." I know there is always a reason. I always stop the attack immediately for them, but then we need to find out why it happened and take steps to make sure it does not happen again.

FIND BLESSED PEOPLE

When I met Mary, even though I did not know anything about BLESSINGS and CURSES at that time, I could sense that God's BLESSING was on her. Eventually I became BLESSED BY God. I think being married to her was definitely a factor. Actually, a huge factor.

I would recommend that you develop relationships with BLESSED people and stay away from people who are CURSED.

Years ago, I was friends with an Air Force Colonel. He had been an aid to a Four-Star General. He maintained a close personal relationship with the General and eventually became a Four-Star General himself. I was BLESSED with great favor in my Air Force career because of my relationship with him, and his relationship with the General.

Proverbs 13:20 people who associate with wise people shall become wise, but a companion of fools shall be destroyed.

Now my life is BLESSED because of my relationship with a BLESSED MINISTER, a BLESSED WIFE AND FAMILY, a BLESSED CHURCH AND BLESSED PRAYER PARTNERS. Are you starting to get the idea that I surround myself with BLESSED PEOPLE?

I do not associate with CURSED PEOPLE! I love them and I minister to them, but I do not hang out with them.

Lot was greatly BLESSED because of his relationship with Abraham and he became very rich. He became CURSED and lost everything he had when he left THE BLESSED MAN and moved in with CURSED, sinful people, the Canaanites. I tell people, "Stay where you are being BLESSED."

Rahab was living in Jericho at the time the Israelites were crossing into the Promised Land. She assisted them in capturing the city and became BLESSED herself. She became the Mother of Ruth's Husband, Boaz and great, great grandmother of King David and is in the line of people that led to the birth of Jesus.

Ruth married Boaz, a BLESSED, covenant person and became BLESSED because she was his wife. She eventually became the great grandmother of King David and is also in the line of people that led to the birth of the Lord Jesus.

When you marry a person who is CURSED, you are bringing the CURSE into your life. When you marry a BLESSED person, you bring the BLESSING into your life.

When the children of Israel went into the promised land, God commanded them to kill every person and animal that could harbor evil spirits. God did not want them to develop relationships with, or even associate with CURSED PEOPLE, or animals that were harboring unclean spirits.

GENERATIONAL CURSES

Deuteronomy 30:19 I call heaven and earth to record what you decide here today. I have set before you, life and death, blessing and cursing, therefore choose life that both you and <u>your descendants</u> may live.

Have you ever wondered why so many people, who live hard lives of sin, sickness and poverty, come from families who lived the same way? Many of the problems in the lives of people today are caused by GENERATIONAL CURSES.

No matter how they start, CURSES can extent in families for thousands of years in the form of GENERATIONAL CURSES.

Most of the sin in the world today, along with sickness, disease, poverty and the hard life has been passed down through families in the form of GENERATIONAL CURSES.

BLESSINGS are generational and so are CURSES. We get to decide which one of the two we will have for ourselves and our descendants. I decided that I am BLESSED and so are my descendants.

Many CURSES are generational and will be passed down the family line for hundreds or even thousands of years. They affect succeeding generations of a family and **all** who come into relationship with members of that family. That is why you should always marry a BLESSED PERSON.

If you made a mistake and married a person affected with GENERATIONAL CURSES, do everything you can to get those broken and to get THE BLESSING to come upon your spouse. We can help you with that.

It seems that any CURSE can become a GENERATIONAL CURSE. Even something as simple as common colds, because some families seem to be more susceptible to colds than others.

The difference between a CURSE and a GENERATIONAL CURSE is that CURSES are only associated with the person involved, but GENERATIONAL CURSES have been passed down in families from previous generations and unless broken, will continue down the line and affect descendants long after the person who is affected now, is gone.

If you have the same problems and difficulties as your parents, or your siblings, you can be sure that there are GENERATIONAL CURSES operating in your life.

CHARACTERISTICS OF GENERATIONAL CURSES

Chronic sickness and disease that runs in families.

Poor people, who come from poor families.

It seems that GENERATIONAL CURSES increase in strength and destruction from one generation to the next down the line. I have noticed that just in our own country, the generation of young people today are worse off, health wise and financially than their parents and grandparents were.

MY FINANCES

For many years my finances were under a GENERATIONAL CURSE but we were always able to use our FAITH to get enough money to pay our bills by the end of the month. I am sure that my grandfather CURSED my father and told him something to the effect that because of a major decision he had made, he would never be successful. His finances were CURSED, but his brothers were very successful. That CURSE was passed down to me, the oldest son, but did not affect my younger brother.

Every month we struggled to come up with enough money to pay our bills. It was a vicious cycle and it went on month after month and year after year. I am sure that many of you know exactly what I am talking about. But, when the GENERATIONAL CURSE of poverty was broken over my life, things began to change. God began to show me that I needed to increase my FAITH and receive THE BLESSING OF ABRAHAM. Now we live in abundance. Please do not be deceived by how simple this is.

MULTIPLE CURSES

Mark 16:9 Now when Jesus rose early the first day of the week, he appeared first to Mary Magdalene, out of whom He had cast seven devils.

I am quite sure that the seven devils got in to her through CURSES.

Many people have several different types of ailments and diseases going on at the same time.

People can have MULTIPLE CURSES. We see that in people who are both sick and broke. I know of many people, including Ministers, who suffer from MULTIPLE CURSES.

There are different types of CURSES and unclean spirits for every type of problem, sickness, and forms of poverty and lack, but all are subject to the Name of Jesus.

LINES OF SPIRITUAL AUTHORITY

In order to break any CURSE and remove accompanying unclean spirits, the lines of authority must be strictly adhered to. It certainly seems that God will not permit the crossing of the authority lines.

Every person, over the age of consent, has spiritual authority over themselves and can break CURSES in their own body, or life. They can also speak good things over themselves. If they do not have strong enough faith, they can **delegate authority** to someone who has stronger faith to do it for them.

We had a case where a young boy was severely oppressed, rolling around on the floor and making terrible noises. His mother brought him to us but the unclean spirit would not obey and come out of him. I told his mother to have the boy's father, who was in another country, call me. The next day he called and I ask him what he wanted me to do. He replied, "Pease heal my son." That evening the boy was totally healed and is now living a normal life.

When you present yourself to someone to be ministered to, you are actually delegating **spiritual authority** to them to do what you need to have done.

People call me every day and tell me what they need from God. By calling, they are giving me the authority to make it happen in their life and I do just that.

Read through the Gospels, Jesus always operated within the spiritual lines of authority when ministering to people. In Matthew 8:8 the Centurion delegated the authority to Jesus to "Speak the Word only" over his servant and heal him.

However, according to Acts 16:16-18 If a demonic spirit is bothering you, through another person, you can cast it out of them, or bind it, if you have GREAT FAITH IN THE NAME OF JESUS.

BREAK THE CYCLE

Breaking the CURSE breaks the cycle of sickness and poverty.

You may have GENERATIONAL CURSES operating in your life that were started 1,000 years ago and were never broken.

BLESSINGS AND CURSES replace each other. If either one is removed it will immediately be replaced by the other.

There is a huge difference between A CURSE and THE CURSE OF THE LAW. There is also a huge difference between **A** BLESSING and **THE** BLESSING OF ABRAHAM.

If for any reason A BLESSING is removed, A CURSE will immediately replace it

If THE BLESSING OF ABRAHAM is removed, the entire CURSE OF THE LAW will immediately replace it. AND, if the entire CURSE OF THE LAW is broken, the entire BLESSING OF ABRAHAM will immediately replace it. How simple is this?

ADOPTED CHILDREN

A very difficult area to talk about is adopted children. I have known many cases of terrible behavior in these children and nothing has seemed to help. We have attempted many times to come against the GENERATIONAL CURSES that these adopted children brought with them from their biological parents, especially their fathers, but, we have never had any success. It seems that spiritual authority to break CURSES does not come along with the adoption of a child. I personally know of one family who had to divorce their adopted child because they were afraid of him.

I know that these children need loving homes and people have a desire to adopt and love a child, but please be careful. If possible, it would be a good idea to investigate the background of a child you are considering for adoption.

STEP CHILDREN

This is another sensitive area where people have had incredible problems. Step children often bring GENERATIONAL CURSES that have been passed down from their biological fathers and these can be very difficult to overcome. Here again, it seems that the step father does not have the same spiritual authority as the biological father.

THE CURSE OF THE LAW

I have heard many people say that Christians cannot have CURSES, or that they cannot be CURSED. All I can say, is read Deuteronomy 28:15-68, which is THE CURSE OF THE LAW, word for word, and then look around at the people the next time you are in church.

Galatians 3:13-14 Christ has redeemed us from the CURSE OF THE LAW because He took the CURSE upon Himself for us so that the BLESSING OF ABRAHAM can come upon the Gentiles through Jesus Christ.

This is what we call the **divine exchange**. Jesus took our sin and gave us His righteousness.

The reason Jesus redeemed us was so that we can be eligible for THE BLESSING OF ABRAHAM, along with the Jewish people.

But unfortunately, THE CURSE OF THE LAW has come back upon most of God's people through sin, disobedience, GENERATIONAL CURSES and SPOKEN WORDS.

The entire CURSE OF THE LAW, word for word, is found in Deuteronomy 28:15-68. Everything in those verses are CURSES. Jesus redeemed us from all of them, which means that we do not have to have any of them. However, these CURSES have found their way back into the lives of many of God's people, mostly because of people CURSING themselves and sin.

You can have the entire CURSE OF THE LAW operating in your life, or you can have portions of it operating in specific designated areas. The latter is more likely.

Even though Jesus has redeemed us, please read Deuteronomy 28:15-68 very carefully. If you see anything in there operating in your life, such as sickness, poverty, lack, a hard life failure, loss or fear, you can be sure that portions of the CURSE OF THE LAW are present in your life. Several years ago, I saw portions of it in my life and that was when I resolved to break it and live in THE BLESSING instead.

God is not actually CURSING the people in Deuteronomy 28:15-68. What He is doing is allowing the CURSE to operate because of disobedience to the law of Moses.

THE BLESSING BLOCKER

The CURSE OF THE LAW is the major BLESSING BLOCKER. I call it the "Mountain" in the lives of people. As long as the CURSE OF THE LAW is in your life, THE BLESSING OF ABRAHAM will be blocked out. However, when the CURSE is removed, THE BLESSING immediately comes in to your life and **if you watch your words,** everything will begin to change for the better.

CURSES OF SICKNESS

Sickness is a major part of THE CURSE OF THE LAW and is oppression of the devil. Sickness is actually one of the punishments for the original sin of Adam.

1 Peter 2:24 by the stripes of Jesus you were healed.

Jesus redeemed us from sickness, by becoming sick Himself, from the beating He took before He went to the cross.

All oppression, including sickness, is subject to THE NAME OF JESUS and can be broken by someone who has GREAT FAITH in that Name.

All CURSES OF SICKNESS cause destruction to the body, which is the Temple of The Holy Ghost.

THE CURSE OF SICKNESS gives different types of accompanying spirits of infirmity a legal right to oppress people and cause sickness and disease.

Spirits of infirmity cannot operate illegally in the body of any person. They must accompany a CURSE OF SICKNESS. In other words, they must be allowed in.

James 2:25 the body without the spirit is dead.

All sickness, disease and infections, including cancer, have unclean spirits living inside of them. Doctors will tell you that cancer, tumors and infections have a life of their own.

All living organisms, no matter where they are living, have a spirit of some kind inside of them. The spirits that live inside of cancer, sickness, disease and infections are evil. The Bible calls these, spirits of infirmity or sickness. These spirits always accompany CURSES OF SICKNESS and because of these CURSES, they have a legal right to be there.

When the CURSE OF SICKNESS is broken and the spirit of infirmity is cast out, the disease will die and will no longer be able to harm a person's body. Once the evil spirit is cast out of cancer, it will quickly die and the body will absorb it. That is how we easily get so many people with cancer healed.

Breaking THE CURSE, or GENERATIONAL CURSE OF SICKNESS removes the legal right for unclean spirits of infirmity to be there and they will not be allowed to return. Healing the sick is a form of deliverance.

Acts 10:38 Jesus healed all who were oppressed of the devil.

Jesus cast evil spirits out of sick people and they healed very quickly. In Luke chapter 13 Jesus cast the spirit of infirmity out of a woman, whom Satan had bound for 18 years, and then He healed her. He also said in verse 16 that Satan had bound the woman for eighteen years. Jesus blamed Satan for the woman's physical problem.

I get people healed the same way. I break the CURSE or GENERATIONAL CURSE that gives the spirits of infirmity a legal right to oppress the person and then I cast out the spirit of infirmity in THE NAME OF JESUS. I then speak to their body and say, "Be healed in THE NAME OF JESUS." This works every single time. If people then watch their words, the cancer, or whatever type of sickness they had, will never come back.

I have had many people with terminal cancer healed. Some of those were so far along in the dying process that they were gasping for breath. I break the CURSE and tell the spirit of death to leave and the spirit inside the cancer to come out. I then lay hands on the person and command their body to be healed in THE NAME OF JESUS. This works every time for me because I have GREAT FAITH IN THE NAME OF JESUS.

The indication that CURSES of sickness are present are chronic illnesses. If they have been running down through families you can be sure that GENERATIONAL CURSES OF SICKNESS are in operation.

THE RIGHTS OF SICKNESS

I have heard many Ministers say that sickness has no right to be in a person's body because our body is the temple of the Holy Ghost. Our body is indeed the Temple of the Holy Ghost, but so many people have given CURSES OF SICKNESS permission to be in their bodies. That gives sickness a legal right to be there.

CURSES OF SICKNESS give unclean spirits a legal right to cause sickness in people. In order to get people healed, we must first take away the legal right for sickness to be there. Breaking the CURSE OF SICKNESS removes the legal right for sickness and disease to grow inside the body of a person.

Medicines, such as antibiotics, chemo and radiation will sometimes kill tumors and infections, but they do not remove the legal right for CURSES OF SICKNESS to be there. That is a huge reason the rate of relapse is so high.

CURSES and unclean spirits of sickness cannot be in a person's life illegally. They must somehow have acquired a legal right, or permission to be there.

Once a CURSE OF SICKNESS is broken, the accompanying unclean spirits will leave with it because they no longer have a legal right to be there.

According to Jesus in Matthew 12:43-45, unclean spirits will try to return to the person they were cast out of. They consider that person to be their home. This includes unclean spirits of infirmity, or sickness. If the CURSE they were accompanying has been broken and the person, who was oppressed, watches their words and does not CURSE themselves again, these unclean spirits of sickness will not be able to return and cause a relapse of the illness.

Another word of warning. I never tell people what to do, or make decisions for them. However, so many times, people are healed through the power of God and told by doctors that they are now cancer free. Then the same doctors, along with members of their families, will convince them to undergo an aggressive treatment plan, "Just to make sure that there is no cancer left." Within a short period of time, the patient is so sick from the treatment, that they start to depend on the doctor and the cancer returns, only much worse this time.

Nineteen years ago, the husband of a woman, in our church, had colon cancer which had spread to his lymph nodes. After surgery, she had me speak healing over him. The doctors soon afterwards told him he was cancer free but they wanted to do a full treatment plan of chemo just to make sure. After only one treatment, he told them that if he was cancer free, he was not going to get any more treatments. He just celebrated his 90th birthday last month and is still in good health.

Jeremiah 17:5 Cursed is the person who depends on another person.

Depending on anyone, for anything, is implied in this verse. God will not BLESS anyone, in any area of their life, when that person is depending on another person, or anything else, to take care of them, or to provide healing for them.

It has been my experience that when a person has looked to the doctors to guarantee their healing, by doing more treatments after they have been healed, the CURSE OF SICKNESS and accompanying unclean spirits of infirmity have always come back.

We have a large list of people who were told by the doctors that they have no trace of cancer left in their bodies but after more treatment, died of cancer that came back in a different place. I believe the new cancer was caused by the same evil spirits of infirmity, that came back with 7 of their even more evil friends, just as Jesus had warned might happen. Matthew 12:43-45

We believe in going to the doctor and it is certainly alright to let the doctor treat the symptoms, but just make sure you are depending on God to heal you and keep your healed.

THE MEDICINE TRAP DEPENDING ON PILLS

It sure seems that the Medical Community is very interested in getting as many people as possible on medicine of some kind. They start with children, diagnosing them with Attention Deficit Hyperactivity Disorder (ADD or ADHD).

Then they want to start them on Ritalin, or some other mind-altering drug. When my son was in 4th grade they wanted him to be on this medicine because they said, "He couldn't pay attention in class." I told them I would not do that as he was a normal, active 10-year-old. I was right, he turned out just fine.

It is certainly alright to take your medicine. Just make sure you do not start to depend on the medicine, instead of God, for your healing and wellbeing.

GENERATIONAL CURSES OF SICKNESS

Every chronic illness is caused by a CURSE of some kind. Most of them are GENERATIONAL CURSES. Examples of these GENERATIONAL CURSES are heart disease, high blood pressure, diabetes, cancer, arthritis, mental illness and dementia.

That is the reason that doctors always want to know if certain diseases run in your family. They call these diseases, hereditary. If you have heart disease and your father had heart disease, the doctor will say that it is hereditary and that will help him, or her with the treatment plan. We call these diseases, generational.

Every sickness, or disease that is passed down in families is generational and could have started hundreds or even thousands of years ago.

Once CURSES OF SICKNESS and GENERATIONAL CURSES OF SICKNESS are broken, and unclean spirits of infirmity are cast out, the person will always heal. Sometimes very quickly and some-times over a period of time, but healing always comes.

CURSES OF POVERTY

Deuteronomy 28:29 You shall grope around at noon like a blind person gropes in darkness and you shall not prosper

in your ways and shall be only oppressed and ruined <u>forever</u> and no person shall be able to help you.

This is part of the CURSE OF THE LAW.

The word **forever**, in this verse, means that this is a GENERATIONAL CURSE OF POVERTY. It is characterized by a chronic lack of sufficiency in all things, especially finances.

2 Corinthians 8:9 For you know the grace of our Lord Jesus Christ, that although He was rich, yet for your sakes He became poor, that we through His poverty can become rich.

Jesus redeemed us from poverty by becoming poor Himself when He was stripped of everything He owned and hung on a cross. Unfortunately, the CURSE OF POVERTY has gotten back into the lives of many people.

The indication that CURSES OF POVERTY are in operation, is chronic financial problems.

Psalm 35:27 Let the Lord be magnified who has pleasure in the prosperity of His servant.

Poverty is never a BLESSING in disguise. God is never glorified by poverty and poverty is never the will of God for anyone.

John 10:10 Jesus said, "I have come so that people can have life and have it more abundantly."

Abundance is always a BLESSING and poverty is always a CURSE.

Poverty is having less than you need on a continuous basis.

The CURSE OF POVERTY causes destruction to finances, which leads to destruction of families and that is its primary intention.

THE BLESSING AND THE CURSE ARE OPPOSITES

Proverbs 10:22 The BLESSING OF THE LORD, it makes people rich and God adds no hard work, or toil with it.

The CURSE OF THE LAW makes people poor and the devil adds hard work and toil to it.

GENERATIONAL CURSES OF POVERTY

Poverty that runs in families is always a GENERATIONAL CURSE.

Almost all poverty is caused by GENERATIONAL CURSES OF POVERTY. Some poverty is caused by bad financial decisions, but that type of poverty is almost always temporary.

Have you ever noticed that almost all poor people come from poor families and almost all rich people come from rich families?

If a poor person had poor parents and grandparents, there is a GENERATIONAL CURSE OF POVERTY involved. This will operate down through the generations of that family until it is removed. This explains why money, no matter how much is spent on poor people, does not solve the problem of poverty.

CURSES of poverty will always give unclean spirits of poverty and spirits of lack, failure and frustration, a legal right to operate in the life of an affected person.

Families who cannot pay their bills experience an incredible amount of stress in their lives.

According to Proverbs 31:7 Poverty is misery and according to Proverbs 28:22 poverty is a spirit.

Because of Malachi 3:8-9, I do not believe that THE CURSE OF POVERTY can be broken from the life of any person who does not tithe.

Poverty is oppression of the devil.

All oppression, including poverty, is subject to THE NAME OF JESUS and can be broken by someone who has GREAT FAITH in that Name.

When I got a revelation that I had a GENERATIONAL CURSE OF POVERTY operating in my life, I went outside on the street at midnight and said, "In the Name of Jesus I break this GENERATIONAL CURSE OF POVERTY that is on my life." Immediately, I could physically feel a wet blanket being pulled up and lifted off of me. I felt light and free of a weight I did not even know I had been carrying. A few months later, things begin to change and now we live in abundance.

CURSE OF THE HARD LIFE

Genesis 3:17-19 And unto Adam he said, Because you have hearkened unto the voice of your wife, and have eaten of the tree, which I commanded you, saying, Thou shalt not

eat of it: cursed is the ground because of you; in sorrow (toil and hard work) shalt you eat of it all the days of your life; ¹⁸ Thorns also and thistles shall it bring forth to you; and you shall eat the vegetables of the field. Verse 19 you shall work to earn a living by the sweat of your face.

Thorns are a sign of THE CURSE OF THE HARD LIFE. Jesus redeemed us from that CURSE OF THE HARD LIFE by wearing a crown of thorns on His Head when He went to the cross. Matthew 27:29.

The CURSE OF THE HARD LIFE is part of THE CURSE OF THE LAW and is oppression of the devil. It is characterized by sweating, Genesis 3:19, while performing hard labor for low wages.

GENERATIONAL CURSE OF A HARD LIFE

Almost all people who work hard with little pay, just to earn enough money to live on, come from parents and grandparents who lived the same way.

Most people in this world live a hard life, working and sweating for little money. These people usually wind up with nothing to show for all of their hard work. My father was one of them. He was completely worn out by the time he was 65 years old. He died sick, with very little to show for all of his hard work except for a nice bright, shiny, red granite tombstone.

Almost all of the neighbors I grew up around, came to the end of their life the same way. Good hard-working people who ended up with little or nothing to leave to their children.

All oppression, including the hard life, is subject to THE NAME OF JESUS and can be broken by someone who has GREAT FAITH in that Name.

CURSE OF FEAR

Deuteronomy 28:66 You will not be sure of keeping your life and you will be afraid day and night and you will even be afraid of everything that you see.

This is part of the CURSE OF THE LAW.

2 Timothy 1:7 God has not given us the spirit of fear, but of power and of love and of a sound mind.

This CURSE of fear seems to be accompanied by a dominate spirit of fear, who will bring with it spirits of worry, anxiety and depression. This CURSE is usually self-imposed by people who say things like, "I am so afraid."

Sickness and poverty are often accompanied by fear, stress and worry, which is a form of doubt, because people are not sure how things are going to turn out. Anxiety and depression come because people do not have FAITH that their situation will ever get better.

One of the worst possible things a person can ever do is to speak fear. Doing so will allow the devil and CURSES access into your life. This results in all kinds of unclean spirits causing major problems for people. Read Job chapter 1.

CURSES OF FAILURE AND LOSS

All failures and loss are part of The CURSE OF THE LAW and is oppression of the devil.

This CURSE is characterized by people failing in business ventures and losing money on "Sure bets." When I was under this CURSE, I would lose money on just about everything I tried to do. Every time I got anything ahead or had something nice, something would happen to take it away, or someone would steal it from me.

Not anymore! That CURSE went away when the CURSE OF THE LAW was broken.

All CURSES OF FAILURE AND LOSS are subject to THE NAME OF JESUS and can be broken by someone who has GREAT FAITH in that Name.

JESUS DID NOT LEAVE US DEFENSELESS

No CURSE within THE CURSE OF THE LAW can stand up to a person who has GREAT FAITH in THE NAME OF JESUS.

Praying is wonderful, but praying does not remove THE CURSE OF THE LAW.

A person with FAITH will fight against CURSES and UNCLEAN SPIRITS and will prevail in battles against them. A person with GREAT FAITH will tell them to leave in THE NAME OF JESUS and that will be the end of it.

Breaking, or removing THE CURSE OF THE LAW will also, at the same time, remove the CURSE OF SICKNESS, the CURSE OF POVERTY, the CURSE OF THE HARD LIFE and THE CURSES OF FAILURE, LOSS AND FEAR.

HELP WITH YOUR FAITH

You can live your life completely CURSE FREE and with the fullness of THE BLESSING OF ABRAHAM if you have GREAT FAITH in THE NAME OF JESUS.

If you yourself have GREAT FAITH in THE NAME OF JESUS, you can use your authority to break THE CURSE OF THE LAW in your life and in your family. If you do not have GREAT FAITH, you can delegate your authority to someone who does have that kind of FAITH, to do it for you. A great example of this in the Bible, is the Centurion in Matthew chapter 8, who ask Jesus to "Speak the Word only" over his servant because he did not have the FAITH to do it himself.

Because Jesus gave us power of attorney to use His Name, no one should ever be living under THE CURSE OF THE LAW.

SIN CURSES

Twice, Jesus said to people, "Go and sin no more." The first person was a sick man. Jesus said to him, "Sin no more, least a worse thing come unto you."

The second person was a woman caught in the act of adultery. Jesus said to her, "Neither do I condemn you, go and sin no more."

In both cases, I am quite sure that Jesus did not expect them to go and live a perfect life. He meant for them to not go back to living a sinful lifestyle. There is a huge difference between making a mistake, or even many of them, and deciding to live a sinful life.

CURSES OF SICKNESS or POVERTY can be caused by unrepentant sin that has come under God's Judgement.

1 Corinthians 5:5 Paul told the Corinthians to turn a person over to Satan for the destruction of the flesh, so that his spirit may be saved.

In 1 Timothy 1:20 Paul told Timothy that he had turned two more people over to Satan, so they would learn not to blaspheme.

CURSES, caused by sin, have been allowed by God, not caused by God. When people repent, these CURSES will go away.

2 Samuel 12:13 David said to Nathan, I have sinned against the Lord and Nathan said to David, "The Lord also has put away your sin, you shall not die."

David avoided the CURSE OF DEATH for his sin because he admitted his sin and repented.

To repent of your sins and ask Jesus to be your Savior will automatically and immediately break the CURSE OF SIN AND DEATH in the life of anyone. No deliverance is necessary.

1 Corinthians 11:31-32 If we judge ourselves, we will not be judged by God. But if we don't judge ourselves, we will be chastened by the Lord so that we will not be condemned with the world.

When God judges a person for sin, CURSES will be allowed to come upon that person. However, God will usually give a person a certain amount of time to judge themselves and repent. If they do that, they will be forgiven, God will not judge them, and no CURSE will be allowed to come upon them. God is so good to us and I am very grateful for that.

Any CURSE that comes in through sin will leave when a person repents of their sin and asks God for forgiveness.

A very well know Pastor of a mega church brought the CURSE OF SICKNESS UPON HIMSELF and died of cancer because he refused to acknowledge and repent of his sins. If he had repented, he could have been healed. If you are sick and not receiving healing, make sure there is no sin in your life.

Unrepentant sin eventually brings God's judgement and that can be a terrible thing. However, according to the above verses, if we judge ourselves and repent for sin, we will not be judged by God.

SINS OF THE FATHER

There is definitely a connection between sins of the father and GENERATIONAL CURSES. It sure seems that fathers who live a sinful lifestyle will have children who live in sin and usually it is the same kind of sin. It becomes a cycle and is passed down through generations.

According to Jeremiah 32:18, Exodus 20:5 and Hosea 4:6 children will suffer for the sins of their fathers. However, the minute a person repents and receives Jesus as their Savior, that cycle of sin is broken.

This cycle can also be stopped by repenting and breaking the CURSE OF SIN in THE NAME OF JESUS.

HOW TO BECOME SAVED

Jesus redeemed us from the CURSE OF SIN. Now all we need to do is repent of our sin and ask Jesus to come into our heart and be our Savior and we can be free from THE CURSE OF SIN.

Repent of the sins of your fathers by saying, "Father God, in the name of Jesus, I repent for my sins, the sins of my fathers and mothers and all of the sins passed down to me. I break every GENERATIONAL CURSE OF SIN in my life. I thank you for total forgiveness. Lord Jesus, please come into my heart right now and be my Savior and I will serve you for the rest of my life.

Renounce the sins of your fathers and your own sin, accept God's forgiveness and forgive yourself. You will be amazed by how your life will change.

CURSES OF DISOBEDIENCE

The children of Israel died in the wilderness because they disobeyed God and would not cross the river into the promised land.

Numbers 14:29 Your carcasses shall fall in the wilderness, everyone twenty years old and up who have disobeyed Me.

Doubt and unbelief led to disobedience and kept the Children of Israel in the wilderness for forty years, where most of them died. Make a decision to believe God's Word and you will never have this problem.

CURSE ON FINANCES

Malachi 3:8-9 Will a person rob God? Yet you have robbed me. But ye say, how have we robbed you? In tithes and offerings. ⁹ Ye are cursed with a curse: for you have robbed me, even this whole nation.

Not tithing brings a CURSE on finances which cannot be broken unless a person begins to tithe. However, tithing alone does not break the CURSE OF POVERTY if it is operating in a person's life. That is why so many people who tithe stay broke and do not increase. The good news is that if you do tithe, the CURSE on your finances can easily be broken.

We tithed for years and stayed broke until we broke the CURSE OF POVERTY over our finances.

Malachi 3:10 Bring all the tithe into the storehouse so that My House is provided for and test Me right now says The Lord, to see if I will open the windows of Heaven and pour out a BLESSING so big for you that you will not have enough room for it.

Tithing is a supernatural transaction and it gives you the right to talk to God about your finances. You can plead your case and even demand that God BLESS you and increase your finances as per Isiah 43:26 where God says, "Remind Me, plead your case, that you may be justified"

Proverbs 3:9-10 Honor the Lord with all the first fruits of your increase. So, shall your barns (storage and bank accounts) be filled with plenty.

Tithing honors God and not tithing dishonors God. If you are tithing, God is obligated to fill your barns, (Bank account).

IDOL WORSHIP

Exodus 20:3 You shall have no other Gods more important to you than Me.

Idol worship is making anything or anyone more important to you than God, or depending on anyone or anything more than you depend on God.

We should always have a list of priorities in our life and God should always be at the very top of this list.

Jeremiah 17:5 Cursed is the person who looks to and depends on other people for anything, instead of completely depending on God.

God demands that we, as His people, depend on Him as our complete source for everything and He absolutely refuses to BLESS anyone who doesn't.

Philippians 4:19 But my God shall supply all of your needs according to His riches in Glory by Christ Jesus.

Depending on your job or other people for money will cause your finances to be CURSED. Depending on the doctors for your healing will cause God to step back and not be involved in your healing. God demands that we consider Him as our only source for all of our needs and wants.

Haggai 1:3-8 be concerned first about building the Lord's house, so that your pockets don't have holes in them to spill out all of your money.

When the CURSE comes in through disobedience it will only leave through repentance and obedience.

SPOKEN CURSES

These are CURSES that have been spoken over a person by themselves, or by someone who has spiritual authority. No one can CURSE you unless they are in a position of spiritual authority over you.

Joshua 6:26 Joshua spoke a CURSE over anyone who would try to rebuild Jericho. He said it would cost them their firstborn in the foundation and their youngest as they set up the gates. 500 years later in 1 Kings 16:34 it happened exactly as he had spoken. The man who rebuilt Jericho lost his oldest and youngest sons in the process.

People cannot CURSE you with their words unless they have spiritual authority over you.

People who practice the occult, cannot put CURSES, or hexes on you. The truth of the matter is this: people who practice different occults have no power at all. They just think they do. The only supernatural power is **The Holy Spirit, THE NAME OF JESUS and the Power of God.**

Numbers 23:8 Balaam was not able to CURSE the children of Israel because they were BLESSED by God and he was not in a position of authority over them.

YOU CAN CURSE YOURSELF

Proverbs 18:21 Your tongue has the power of life and death over you and you will live by the words that you speak.

You can BLESS YOURSELF, or CURSE YOURSELF, depending on what words you speak about yourself.

As a matter of fact, **every time** you say something about yourself, you either BLESS YOURSELF, or CURSE YOURSELF.

James 3:2 If any person does not CURSE themselves with their words, they are a mature person and able to control their life.

If you watch your words you will not CURSE YOURSELF and give the devil and unclean spirits a legal right to come into your life and cause destruction.

Wrong words can activate a CURSE, without sin being involved. Even people living a good life, free of sin, can be CURSED or CURSE THEMSELVES.

CURSING CHILDREN

Genesis 9:25 And Noah said to his son, Ham, "Cursed be Canaan, a servant of servants you shall be to your brethren."

When Noah CURSED his son Ham, he gave the devil permission to keep him and all of his descendants as servants. However, that CURSE, just like any other CURSE, can be broken.

Most CURSES operating in the lives of people, are there as a result of someone CURSING themselves with their words, or by someone else CURSING them who has the spiritual authority to speak CURSES over them, such as their parents. The worst thing a parent can do is to call their child stupid or to tell them, "You will never amount to anything."

Please understand this, **YOUR CHILD WILL BECOME WHAT YOU CALL THEM.** If you call them smart, they will be smart. Never say, "You are a bad boy, or girl" unless you want to have a bad child.

How many times have you heard people say bad things to, or about their children? Such as: my son is not smart, my kids have no ambition, they will never amount to anything, my kids get sick all the time. These SIMPLE CURSES will turn into GENERATIONAL CURSES.

PEOPLE UNWITTINGLY CURSE CHILDREN

I know a man who called his son, "Clown" as the child was growing up. The boy looked like and acted like a clown. He is now grown with a family of his own and he still looks and acts like a clown.

I used to smoke years ago, and one day as I was lighting up a cigarette I said to my father, "I am going to quit smoking." He looked at me and said, "You will smoke until the day you die." I said, "No, I am going to quit." Well, I tried many times but I just could not stop smoking. Even after I was saved and filled with the Holy Ghost, I was still smoking some. I hid my cigarettes because I was embarrassed by what I was doing but I could not stop.

Finally, one day I was listening to a Derrick Prince tape about CURSES and the Lord showed me a vision of my father CURSING me concerning the smoking. I stood up and said, "In THE NAME OF JESUS I break that CURSE my father spoke over me about smoking until the day I die."

I went back to my desk and lit up a cigarette. But, two weeks later the urge to smoke was gone and I just stopped. I have never smoked again nor had the urge to. Praise God. My father had not meant me any harm, he just did not know any better.

CURSING PETS

Many people CURSE their pets by saying things like, "My dog is stupid, my dog runs away every chance he gets, my cat hates me." These are CURSES and the pets will behave according to their owner's words. Speak good things and BLESSINGS over your pets and you will have wonderful pets.

DESIGNATED CURSES

Each individual CURSE is for a certain area of a person's life and will not affect other areas. Example: CURSES of sickness will not affect finances and vice versa.

A SPOKEN CURSE is always designated to affect a specific area of someone's life. For example: if you say "My knees hurt all the time" you will have constant pain in your knees, while the rest of your body can remain unaffected. Or, if you say something like "I can't afford a new car" you will never have enough money to buy a new car, but you could have plenty of money for everything else.

All unclean spirits have specific assignments and DESIGNATED SPOKEN CURSES will determine which ones will be allowed into your body and your life.

Proverbs 18:21 Your tongue has the power of life and death over you and you will live by the words that you speak about yourself.

Everyone has the power and authority to keep CURSES and unclean spirits out of their lives, or to let them in.

INSTRUMENT OF AUTHORITY

According to James Chapter 3 your **tongue** will control your body and your life. Also, according to Deuteronomy 30:19 you can choose CURSES or BLESSINGS, life or death. Please read my book, "The Power of Positive Words." This is the second most important book you will ever read.

James 3:10 Out of the same mouth people bless them-selves and curse themselves. This should not be.

Don't give the devil the legal right to send his CURSES and evil spirits into your life, or the lives of your family, with your words.

Mark 11:23 The word mountain in this verse means hinderance or obstacles, which can be the result of a SPOKEN CURSE. God will never remove a SPOKEN CURSE from anyone.

CURSES can start by simply saying things such as, "My arm hurts all the time, I have bad feet, I get migraines, we get sick every time the flu comes around, or everyone in my family has health problems." These will turn into GENERATIONAL CURSES.

PROTECT YOUR BRAIN

99.999% of people with dementia, at one time CURSED their brain by saying, "I can't remember things like I used to, or I am getting forgetful." You can protect your brain by being careful what you say about it. Don't invite CURSES into your brain.

BLESS your brain by speaking positively about it. Say, "I am smart and getting smarter every day, I am quick and sharp and I never forget anything, I have the mind of Christ."

A CURSE can be spoken over a certain body part or area of a person's life. Other areas of their body and life may, at the same time, remained BLESSED. Please be careful with your brain.

DON'T CURSE YOUR HEART

If you CURSE your heart by saying, "I have a bad heart, I guarantee that you will more than likely die of heart disease.

I was visiting a man in the hospital who was suffering from severe heart disease and his son came in. He said to me, "All the men in our family die young with heart problems." I thought to myself, yes and you will to if you don't change what you are saying about yourself.

BLESS your heart by saying, "My heart is strong and getting stronger every day. Bless your lungs the same way and your legs and your back and eyes and the rest of your body. Break every CURSE affecting your body and say every organ and every part of my body works perfectly.

SELF IMPOSED CURSES

Matthew 12:37 Jesus said by the words you speak you either justify yourself or condemn yourself.

Wrong words spoken by you will open your life up to CURSES and unclean spirits.

Most problems in the lives of people are a result of SPOKEN CURSES.

CURSING YOURSELF

The easiest way to CURSE YOURSELF is to say I can't, or something is hard to do.

"I can't afford to pay my rent."" If you say that, you have CURSED your ability to pay your rent.

I cannot begin to tell you how many people I have heard say, "Its just one thing after another." That is a CURSE and it will cause one bad thing after another to happen in their lives.

The worst word you can ever use when talking about yourself is the word **damn**. Never say, "I'll be damned." Instead when something surprises you say, "Well, I'll be BLESSED."

The second worst word, is the word **can't**. If you say, "I can't," you can't.

The third worst word you can say about yourself is **hard**. If you say that something is hard to do, it most certainly will be.

I picked up a wonderful lady one morning for church. As I was opening the door for her to get in, she turned to me and said, "Getting ready on Sunday morning gets harder every time." I got into the car and said, "Why would you say something like that about yourself?" She replied, "I am just telling the truth." A few months later, she was no longer able to get herself ready for church.

God does not remove SPOKEN CURSES and Prayer does not work either.

SPOKEN CURSES can only be removed by someone who has spiritual authority and GREAT FAITH in the Name of Jesus.

The bottom line is this: If you do not control your words you will constantly be plagued with CURSES. If you do control your words you can live a CURSE FREE life and that means you will live A BLESSED ABUNDANT LIFE.

To speak a CURSE over someone under your spiritual authority is to give unclean spirits permission to enter their life in a specific area and cause failure and destruction in that area.

CURSES must always be removed the same way they got in. If they came in through words they must be removed by words. If they were voice activated, such as being spoken by a person in authority, they must be removed by a person in authority. Either you or someone in authority over you must command them to leave.

HOW PEOPLE CURSE THEMSELVES

Partial list of statements that people use to CURSE themselves:

- I can't afford that.

- I never seem to have enough money.

- I can't do that.

- I can't remember things like I used to.

- I must be going crazy.

- I am losing my mind.

- I am so ugly.

- We get the flu every year.

- I always do dumb things.

- Nobody likes me.

- I don't have any friends,

- I am such a klutz.

- I am so stupid.

- I am such a loser.

- Nothing ever works out for me.

- I get sick all the time.

- I can't get over this.

- I have senior moments.

- I can't find a good job.

- This is hard.

- I can't figure this out.

- I can't learn this.

- This always happens to me.

- Its just one thing after another.

Are you starting to get the picture? And, if you agree with any-one who makes these statements, you are also CURSED. See how easy it is to get yourself CURSED?

PEOPLE CURSE THEMSELVES IN CHURCH

Be careful when agreeing with Ministers. I have heard preachers say some horrific things and people in church responding with an amen, which means, so be it. I heard a nationally known Minister say, "Trouble will come to you." People all over the very large church were saying. "Amen." I immediately said, very loudly, "Not to me it won't." When people turned to see who had said that I said, "I am not going to agree with that." Half of the people in that church, probably

2,000 or so, CURSED themselves that Sunday morning and gave the devil permission to bring trouble into their lives, but I didn't.

REMOVING SPOKEN CURSES

SPOKEN CURSES must always be removed by you or by someone in authority over you, issuing a command in THE NAME OF JESUS.

If THE CURSE OF THE LAW was broken in the life of a person and also every GENERATIONAL CURSE and then THE BLESSING was spoken over them and a piece of duct tape put over their mouth and left there, they would live an UNHINDERED BLESSED LIFE.

The bottom line is this: if you control your words you can live a CURSE FREE LIFE.

OTHER TYPES OF CURSES

Step 1. Recognize if any of these CURSES are operating in your life.

Step 2. Break the CURSE in the NAME OF JESUS, or have someone who has GREAT FAITH in that Name do it for you.

Step 3. Make a good confession every day for at least 90 days. This will increase your faith and also, according to Revelation 12:11, a good testimony and confession will reinforce your deliverance from a CURSE.

We need to stop trying to deal with the habits of people and deal with the root cause of their problems.

CURSES NEED FOOD

Many times, CURSES perpetuate addictions to things like nicotine, alcohol, drugs, medicines, caffeine, food, soda, sugar, gambling or other harmful things. CURSES and unclean spirits **need something to feed on** and sin and bad habits are great food for them.

Keep in mind that before any of these CURSES can be broken, and kept out of your life, you must make a firm decision to be rid of sin and any bad habits you might have. **Do not play games with CURSES!**

Most of these CURSES are also GENERATIONAL as they run in families.

- **CURSE OF ALCOHOLISM:** Alcoholic fathers produce alcoholic children. Results in public drunkenness, fighting, family abuse, criminal activity, major liver, stomach, other health problems and loss of employment. Break, then confess, "I do not desire to drink alcohol.

- **CURSE OF SMOKING:** Results in lung disease, cancer and other health problems. Usually shortens life by 10-15 years. Break, then confess every time you light up a cigarette, "I do not desire to smoke." The desire to smoke will leave within 90 days.

- **CURSE OF CHRONIC PAIN:** Millions of people are affected with physical pain that never seems to go away. Narcotics only mask the symptoms and can cause terrible addiction problems. Refuse to accept pain in your life. Break, then confess "I do not have any pain in my body."

- **CURSE OF SUICIDE:** This is almost always a GENERATIONAL CURSE. If there is any history of suicide in your family, or if you have had any thoughts of taking your own life, please get help immediately.

- **CURSE OF GAMBLING:** Results in severe debt, failed relationships, depression, anxiety and mood disorders. Break, then confess, "I do not desire to gamble."

- **CURSE OF DEBT:** Results in extreme stress and harassment by creditors. Break, then confess, "I am debt free and will stay that way."

- **CURSE OF ADULTERY:** Results in breakup of marriages and families. Break, then confess, "I am a faithful husband, or wife."

- **CURSE OF FRUSTRATION:** Results in frustration and stress because of situations and circumstances. Break, then confess, I do not get frustrated because everything works out for me and everyone around me is wonderful.

- **CURSE OF ANGER:** Results in people using anger and mood swings as a means to control other people. Causes loss of relationships and friendships. Break, then confess, "I am a wonderful, friendly person."

- **CURSE OF GLUTTONY:** Results in weight gain and loss of health. Break, then confess, "I do not desire to overeat." This can result in a huge weight loss.

- **CURSE OF BEING ACCIDENT PRONE:** Results in being a danger to yourself and others. Break, then confess, "I am not accident prone and I do not have accidents."

- **CURSE OF STUPIDITY OR FOOLISHNESS:** Results in a lack of good sense, or judgement, making bad decisions. A STUPID CURSE can get started if a person says something like, "Boy am I stupid, or I do stupid things all the time." Break, then confess, "I am smart and getting smarter every day." This confession will actually increase the intelligence of anyone who says it every day.

- **CURSE OF MISCARRIAGES:** Results in a woman not being able to carry a baby to full term. Break, then confess, "I will have a healthy, happy baby." I have broken this CURSE in the lives of two young women. Both had had several miscarriages. They both then had full term healthy babies.

- **CURSE OF FATGUE:** Results in a loss of productivity. Break, then confess, "I have lots of energy."

There are certainly more CURSES but you get the idea. The rule of thumb is this: if it is bad and chronic, it is a CURSE. If it is bad and chronic and runs in families, it is a GENERATIONAL CURSE.

REMOVING CURSES

Jesus does not break THE CURSE OF THE LAW, or CURSES of any kind, nor cast out unclean spirits in the lives of people today. He told us to do that for ourselves in Mark 16:17.

There is only one power on this earth that will remove a CURSE and that is the power in THE **NAME** OF JESUS.

When Jesus was dying on the cross He said "It is finished." What he meant was that He had paid the entire penalty for sin and redeemed mankind from THE CURSE OF THE LAW.

All CURSES, no matter what kind they are, must obey commands made IN THE NAME OF JESUS, by a person who is in authority and who has GREAT FAITH in that Name.

If there is active sin, unforgiveness, or willful disobedience in the life of a person, deliverance from CURSES and unclean spirits will not be successful.

There is no force on this earth that will break a CURSE, or remove UNCLEAN SPIRITS, except a command issued by a person who has GREAT FAITH in THE NAME OF JESUS. They must also have authority, direct, or delegated, to do so.

In order to live a CURSE FREE life, you must absolutely refuse to allow any CURSES to operate in your life and have GREAT FAITH in THE NAME OF JESUS, or **have access** to someone, on a regular basis, who does have that kind of FAITH.

The first choice should be your Pastor. If your Pastor is not available, or does not have GREAT FAITH in THE NAME OF JESUS, (Most don't) find someone who does and who is available to you.

THE SIMPLE SECRET

Matthew 17:19-20 Then the disciples came to Jesus and ask why they could not cast out the devil and Jesus told them it was because of their unbelief.

Only someone with GREAT FAITH in THE NAME OF JESUS can remove CURSES and UNCLEAN SPIRITS.

The **SIMPLE SECRET** to breaking CURSES and removing unclean spirits is found in **Mark 16:17. These signs (Miracles) shall follow those people who have FAITH in My Name.**

GREAT FAITH IN THE NAME OF JESUS. Nothing else works! I call this key secret because very few people know about it. GREAT FAITH is necessary to properly break CURSES. Most people who try, end up doing more harm than good in people's lives.

CURSES cannot be overcome, but can quickly be removed by a person who has authority and GREAT FAITH in the Name of Jesus.

If a CURSE is removed from any area of your life, a BLESSING will immediately replace it.

If the entire CURSE OF THE LAW is broken and removed from the life of a person, all of the CURSES associated with it, and all accompanying unclean spirits will leave at the same time. The

entire BLESSING OF ABRAHAM, listed in Deuteronomy 28:1-14, will immediately replace it.

Philippians 2:10 That at the name of Jesus every knee should bow, of things in Heaven, and things in earth, and things under the earth.

This also includes all CURSES and the unclean spirits which accompany CURSES. All CURSES, no matter what type they are, must obey commands made in the NAME OF JESUS, by a person who has GREAT FAITH in that Name.

There is enough power in THE NAME OF JESUS to break every CURSE and GENERATIONAL CURSE in the life of a person, or family, or large group of people, at the same time, with one command.

You can live CURSE FREE with the fullness of THE BLESSING OF ABRAHAM operating in your life, if you, or someone you have access to, has GREAT FAITH in THE NAME OF JESUS and knows how to deal with CURSES.

KEYS OF THE KINGDOM

CURSES and unclean spirits can be bound on earth, by a person who has GREAT FAITH in the Name of Jesus, and it will then be bound from Heaven. Matthew 16:19. Or, they can be loosed from earth, into the body, or life of a person by someone who has spiritual authority, and then they will be loosed from Heaven.

When a CURSE is broken, the accompanying unclean spirits no longer have a legal right to be there and they will leave.

Having GREAT FAITH in THE NAME OF JESUS, or access to someone who does, will allow you to live a life completely unhindered by CURSES and unclean spirits. That is the way God intended for all of us to live and you can live a CURSE FREE LIFE.

ABOUT THE AUTHOR

Pastor Jim Kibler was born in Pittsburgh and grew up in Slippery Rock, Pennsylvania. He is a graduate of Mount St. Mary's College in Emmitsburg, Maryland, and Rhema Bible College in Tulsa, Oklahoma. He also did graduate work in business at George Washington University in Washington, DC.

Pastor Jim and his wife Mary, who is also a graduate of Rhema Bible College, Pastor **Life Church** in Indialantic, Florida.

Pastor Jim's popular website is www.increasenow.com, a **FREE SITE**, where people around the world watch his FREE 15 Minute videos every day. He teaches about God's Goodness, Healing, Redemption, Abundance and The Blessing. Also watch Pastor Jim's live broadcast every day by downloading the free **Periscope App** on your phone and follow Pastor Jim Kibler.

In addition, Pastor Jim is a Very Entertaining Conference Speaker and everywhere he speaks, people get healed, finances increase and churches grow. He makes God's Word very easy to understand. He also has a very anointed healing ministry with people being healed of every type of disease and blind eyes opened.

Pastor Jim has a wonderful Prayer Ministry with Prayer Partners all over the world and makes himself available to pray with people who do not have a Pastor to pray with them. He is Personal Pastor to many people who otherwise do not have a Pastor to Talk to, Speak THE BLESSING over them, or Pray the Prayer of Faith for their needs.

His Prayer Ministry has had incredible results. Many people are healed right over the phone, have the curse of the law and generational curses broken and have THE BLESSING activated in their lives.

Pastor Jim's phone number is available at www.increasenow.com

He is called the **"How To Preacher"** because he not only teaches people what God has promised, but how to receive it.

Other Books by Pastor Jim:

"The Power Of Positive Words"

"Faith"

"How To Pray"

"The Blessing"

"Jesus"

"The Blessing and The Tithe"

"If the Bible Is True"

.

Made in the USA
Columbia, SC
29 September 2019